Malorie Blackman

A Storytelling Sensation

First published in Great Britain in 2015
by Wayland

Copyright © Wayland, 2015

Editor: Elizabeth Brent

Produced for Wayland by Calcium
All rights reserved.
Dewey Number: 823.9'2-dc23
ISBN: 978 0 7502 9043 2
Ebook ISBN: 978 0 7502 9044 9
10 9 8 7 6 5 4 3 2 1

Wayland
An imprint of
Hachette Children's Group
Part of Hodder & Stoughton
Carmelite House
50 Victoria Embankment
London EC4Y 0DZ

An Hachette UK Company
www.hachette.co.uk

www.hachettechildrens.co.uk

Picture acknowledgements:

Key: b=bottom, t=top, r=right, l=left,
m=middle, bgd=background

Cover: Alamy: Steven May 12 (inset); Corbis: Kathy de Witt/Lebrecht
Music & Arts (main). **Inside:** Alamy: Art Directors & TRIP 10b, Kathy
deWitt 9, GL Portrait 17, Steven May 12, WENN Ltd 1; Booktrust:
Johnny Ring 5t, 30; Bromley Local Studies and Archives: 8; Corbis:
Kathy de Witt/Lebrecht Music & Arts 18, Rune Hellestad 22; Getty
Images: Bentley Archive/Popperfoto 7, Evening Standard 6; Helen
Giles: 2, 4, 21, 24; NASA: 11; Penguin Random House Children's
Publisher: 5b, 13, 19l, 19r, 23l, 23r; Rex Features: Jonathan Hordle 26,
Geoffrey Swaine 15; Shutterstock: Aija Lehtonen 26b, Neftali 10t; The
Reading Agency: 29; Wikimedia Commons: York College ISLGP 20.

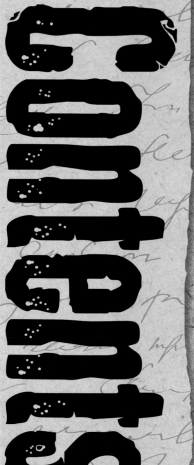

Malorie Blackman

Malorie Blackman:
The Word Wizard

■ Children everywhere love Malorie Blackman's books. They are full of lovable characters, thrilling plots and fantastical themes. Not only does Malorie write great stories, but she has also changed the world of children's fiction.

Before Malorie started writing, most children's novels published in the UK had only white heroes and heroines. Malorie's books are full of dynamic, black characters that are as inspirational as Malorie herself.

'WHAT I HOPE I'M DOING IS PRESENTING POSITIVE IMAGES OF BLACK CHILDREN SIMPLY LIVING, INSTEAD OF COPING WITH A PROBLEM.'

NAME: Malorie Blackman

BORN: 8 February 1962

HOMETOWN: South London, England

SCHOOLS: Churchfields Primary School and Honor Oak Grammar School

OCCUPATION: Children's book author

FAMOUS FOR: Being one of the UK's greatest children's book authors

DID YOU KNOW?

MALORIE BLACKMAN LIVES IN KENT WITH HER HUSBAND, NEIL, AND THEIR DAUGHTER, ELIZABETH. SHE WORKS IN A BACK BEDROOM OF HER HOUSE – IN SILENCE! MALORIE SAYS SHE CANNOT WRITE WHEN DISTRACTED BY NOISE.

What if you had to crack a code to save a life?

A.N.T.I.D.O.T.E

malorie **blackman**

Author of the award-winning NOUGHTS & CROSSES

BARBADOS TO ENGLAND

In 1960, two years before Malorie was born, her parents emigrated from Barbados to England. With few job opportunities in their home country, Malorie's parents made the move to look for work.

The move to England was not an easy one because Malorie's parents already had two children – a boy and a girl. They had to make the difficult decision to leave the children behind until their new life was secure enough to give the family a good home.

Many people emigrated from the Caribbean to England during the 1950s and 1960s in search of better employment opportunities.

Malorie was born in 1962 and, three years later, the family grew again when Malorie's mother discovered that she was expecting twin boys. With family life, work and a home established in England, Malorie's mother and father sent for her elder siblings too, and the family was finally together again.

Growing up in a black family in England in the 1960s was not easy, and Malorie and her family experienced racism from the white community around them. Malorie witnessed how hard it was for black people to get good jobs, and how limited their life opportunities were compared with those of white people. Her early childhood experiences made her determined as an adult to change attitudes towards black people.

MALORIE ON RACISM: 'I THINK A LOT OF RACISM COMES OUT OF IGNORANCE, AND WE CAN START TO COMBAT IT BY SHOWING DIFFERENT CULTURES, RACES, RELIGIONS IN STORY CONTEXTS. STORIES PROMOTE EMPATHY, A SENSE OF BEING ABLE TO SEE THROUGH THE EYES OF OTHERS AND BEING ABLE TO WALK IN ANOTHER PERSON'S SHOES.'

MALORIE'S STORY

WHEN MALORIE WAS GROWING UP, SOCIAL AND ECONOMIC DISADVANTAGE AND DISCRIMINATION MADE IT DIFFICULT FOR BLACK CHILDREN TO ASPIRE TO BE WRITERS. BLACK PEOPLE WERE DISCRIMINATED AGAINST BECAUSE OF THEIR COLOUR AND AS A RESULT FOUND IT DIFFICULT TO GET WELL-PAID JOBS. MALORIE HAS SINCE SPOKEN OUT ABOUT THE LACK OF OPPORTUNITIES FOR BLACK PEOPLE AND THE ATTITUDES TOWARDS THEM: 'BASICALLY, WE WERE CONSIDERED FACTORY FODDER.'

School, Stories and Inspiration

Malorie enjoyed her schooldays at Churchfields Primary School. She loved looking at books, reading them over and over again and collecting her favourites. Malorie spent as much time as she could hunched over storybooks, reading quietly – she often had to be told to stop reading and continue with her other lessons!

Malorie's love of words and reading was clear to her primary school teacher, Miss Jones. Seeing the youngster's passion for books, she encouraged Malorie to start telling stories of her own and to write down her wonderful ideas. Today, Malorie says that Miss Jones was the person who first set her on the path to becoming a children's book author.

At home, Malorie's early childhood was a happy one. She spent her time playing, having fun with her young twin brothers and getting to know her elder brother and sister better.

MALORIE ON HER CHILDHOOD: 'I SPENT MOST SATURDAYS DURING MY EARLY YEARS AT THE LIBRARY, DRINKING IN FAIRY STORIES, MYTHS AND LEGENDS, CLASSICS, CONTEMPORARY STORIES, FANTASY, SCIENCE FICTION AND ANYTHING ELSE I COULD LAY MY HANDS ON.'

Malorie spent many happy hours in her local library, reading all the fiction titles on the shelves!

MALORIE'S STORY

MALORIE'S LOVE OF READING AND COLLECTING BOOKS AS A CHILD HAS CONTINUED INTO ADULTHOOD. SHE NOW HAS AN ENORMOUS STASH OF BOOKS IN HER HOUSE – AN UNBELIEVABLE 10,000 TITLES – AND SHE IS STILL ADDING TO IT!

As an adult, Malorie is determined to help young children find inspiration in books and to write if they want to, or to pursue any other dream. She regularly visits schools across the UK to talk to children about their goals, telling them her own life story: 'I talk about my life and how I got into writing in the first place. I'm keen to point out that if I can do it, anybody can. You can be anything, even president of America, you know!'

MALORIE ON READING: 'I BELIEVE THAT WE HAVE TO GET CHILDREN INTERESTED IN READING FROM THE TIME THEY'RE BORN BY SHOWING THEM HOW READING OPENS SO MANY DOORS. IF A CHILD TELLS ME THEY DON'T LIKE READING, I ALWAYS SAY, "YOU HAVEN'T FOUND THE RIGHT BOOKS FOR YOU YET!"'

'...CHILDREN ARE A DISCERNING AUDIENCE WHOSE MINDS HAVEN'T YET BEEN CLOSED DOWN. AND I LIKE THE WAY CHILDREN ARE HONEST ABOUT WHAT THEY LIKE AND DON'T LIKE.'

A World of Stories

There was hardly a storybook in the school library that Malorie had not read by the time she was eight years old! She especially loved reading fantasy stories about mythical creatures or tales about heroines who triumphed in the end. Some of Malorie's favourite childhood books included *The Chronicles of Narnia, The Silver Chair* and *Rebecca*. She says *The Silver Chair* was her favourite book.

THE CHRONICLES OF NARNIA
THE LION, THE WITCH AND THE WARDROBE
C.S. Lewis

BOOK 2

Malorie also told many stories of her own. Her imagination ran riot and she loved nothing more than making up fanciful tales full of amazing characters and fairy-tale influences.

Along with reading storybooks, Malorie loved watching television programmes that featured fascinating characters from other worlds. Her love of strong characters and fantasy worlds can be seen in many of the stories she has written as an adult. She has described *Star Trek* as inspiring her to write about science fiction – and to see how different races could work harmoniously together: 'I'm a *Star Trek* girl, really – I grew up seeing a black actress playing Uhura on the bridge, and all nationalities working together.'

Boys Don't Cry and *Cloud Busting* are two of Malorie's best-known stories. They both have themes that Malorie loves to use in her writing – computers and technology, and relationships between very different people.

CLOUD BUSTING
THIS AWARD-WINNING BOOK BY MALORIE IS WRITTEN ENTIRELY IN VERSE! IT TELLS THE STORY OF THE FRIENDSHIP BETWEEN A BULLY, SAM, AND A QUIET, THOUGHTFUL BOY NAMED DAVEY.

BOYS DON'T CRY
THIS BOOK LOOKS AT THE TEENAGE DIFFICULTIES OF TWO VERY DIFFERENT BOYS, DANTE AND ADAM, AND HOW THEY STRUGGLE TO COPE WITH LIFE CHANGES AND SOCIETY'S EXPECTATIONS.

At the end of primary school, Malorie passed her 11+ exam and joined Honor Oak Grammar School. It was a huge achievement and, pleased with her success, Malorie settled into life at secondary school. However, things were soon to change.

When Malorie was 13 years old, her world was turned on its head when she came home from school one day to find her father had left home. This came as a terrible shock to Malorie, her mother and her brothers and sister.

Malorie tried to adjust to her new family situation, but she felt very sad. She found comfort in writing down her feelings in her diary and writing poems about her family life. When Malorie was 16, her father moved back in with the family, but stayed only for a short time before he left again. Malorie had to get over the family break-up for a second time. She never saw her father again.

Malorie at a promotional event for her novel *Checkmate*

MALORIE BLACKMAN

Checkmate

'I WROTE OUT ALL THE PAIN, ALL THE FEELINGS I COULDN'T SHARE, IN SECRET POEMS.'

In two of her best-loved stories, Noughts & Crosses and Pig Heart Boy, Malorie talks about how people can overcome racism and prejudice through determination and strength of character.

NOUGHTS & CROSSES
IN THIS BOOK, THE WORLD IS DIVIDED IN TWO, WITH BLACK PEOPLE AS THE SUPERIOR RACE, KNOWN AS CROSSES. WHITE PEOPLE ARE SECOND-CLASS CITIZENS, CALLED NOUGHTS. THE STORY EXAMINES RACIAL PREJUDICE AND DIVISIONS IN SOCIETY.

PIG HEART BOY
THE HERO OF THIS STORY, CAMERON, IS VERY SICK AND NEEDS A NEW HEART. TO SAVE HIM, DOCTORS OFFER TO REPLACE CAMERON'S HEART WITH THAT OF A PIG. CAMERON THEN STRUGGLES TO BE ACCEPTED BY THOSE AROUND HIM BECAUSE OF HIS 'PIG HEART'.

Not only did Malorie have to cope with a family break-up as a teenager, but she was also bullied for being black. Rather than crumbling under the racist attacks, Malorie became determined to fight back by making a success of her life and has since used her experiences of racism and discrimination in her stories.

BLACK AND WHITE RIGHT AND WRONG.

INCLUDES THE SHORT STORY, CALLUM

NOUGHTS & CROSSES

malorie blackman

THE FIRST BOOK IN THE AWARD-WINNING SEQUENCE

A Wrong Turn

As her school life began to draw to a close, Malorie looked to the future and what to do after school. Having always loved reading and writing, she decided to study English at college. She put the idea forward to her school careers advisor, however, Malorie did not get the response she had expected...

Shockingly, Malorie's careers advisor told her that she should not try to study English, saying that her English was not good enough for a degree course! The advisor told Malorie that she should instead apply for a course at Huddersfield Polytechnic in Yorkshire. Believing her careers advisor to be correct, and with her confidence in her abilities shaken, Malorie went ahead and applied for the course. She was accepted and left home to study in Yorkshire.

MALORIE'S STORY

MALORIE ACHIEVED GOOD GRADES AT SCHOOL YET HER CAREERS ADVISER STILL TOLD HER THAT SHE SHOULD NOT APPLY TO READ ENGLISH AT UNIVERSITY. MALORIE MADE SURE, HOWEVER, THAT SHE PASSED HER ENGLISH A LEVEL, WHICH MEANT THAT SHE COULD RETURN TO HER ENGLISH STUDIES LATER IF SHE WANTED TO.

During the first term of her business studies course, Malorie realised that she had made a terrible mistake. Although she loved college life and enjoyed her independence living away from home, she hated the course – and hated that she was not studying English, the subject she loved. Malorie did not know what to do, and did not feel she could confide in her family that she had made a wrong decision.

Today, having learnt from her own experience of being encouraged to follow a path that was not right for her, Malorie urges young people to follow their dreams. She tells them not be deterred by what other people think, believing that following your instincts is the way to true success and happiness. She says, 'If you want something, go for it.'

'I GO TO A BLACK WOMEN'S WRITERS GROUP, AND WE ALL GOT TOLD, "BLACK WOMEN DON'T GO TO COLLEGE." IT'S SUCH INSIDIOUS STUFF. KIDS ARE STILL AMAZED WHEN I WALK IN, AND THEY SEE THAT YOU CAN BE BLACK, AND A WRITER.'

Sickle-Cell SHOCK

Struggling with the knowledge that she had chosen the wrong course at college, Malorie then had further bad news to deal with. One day, while in her college room, she suddenly felt very unwell, with terrible stomach pains. Malorie was rushed to hospital, and sent for an operation to remove her appendix. When she woke up from the general anaesthetic, it was to the doctors and nurses talking about her having a disease called sickle-cell anaemia. Malorie was terrified.

Sickle-cell anaemia, as Malorie later discovered, is a condition common among Afro-Caribbean people. It is a serious disease in which the body makes red blood cells, which look like a crescent, rather than the disc-shaped blood cells found in most people. Healthy blood cells carry oxygen-rich blood around the body, however sickle cells, which are stiff and sticky, block the flow of blood around the body. When the blood flow becomes blocked, it can cause severe pain and damage to internal organs. It can also cause infections.

2:15 AM

MALORIE'S STORY

BEING DIAGNOSED WITH SICKLE-CELL ANAEMIA AND THE EFFECT THAT HAD ON MALORIE, HAS FED THROUGH TO HER STORIES. IN HER BOOK, FORBIDDEN GAME, THE CHARACTER SHAUN HAS SICKLE-CELL ANAEMIA. THROUGHOUT HIS STORY MALORIE SHOWS THE EFFECT THE CONDITION HAS ON THE LIVES OF SUFFERERS.

Malorie spent many months trying to come to terms with the fact that she had a life-threatening condition. However, she later learned that the doctors had wrongly diagnosed her – she didn't have sickle-cell anaemia after all.

Malorie felt very angry for a long time that she had been wrongly diagnosed and made to live with the fear and worry of such a serious condition. However, she has since said that believing she had the condition helped her become even more determined to pursue her dreams. If she had not thought she had sickle-cell anaemia, she may not have made the decisions that led to her becoming a successful author.

MALORIE ON HER INCORRECT DIAGNOSIS: 'FOR YEARS I WAS BITTER AND ANGRY ABOUT IT... ALTHOUGH I KNEW THAT THE DIAGNOSIS WAS FALSE, I'D GOT THE NOTION WELL AND TRULY INTO MY HEAD, AND IT MADE ME REALISE I DIDN'T WANT TO DIE WITHOUT LEAVING SOMETHING BEHIND! NOW I LOOK BACK AND THINK, YES, YOU REALLY DID DO ME A FAVOUR.'

Changing Course

Recovering from her appendix operation in London, still believing she had sickle-cell anaemia and hating her business studies course, Malorie decided to change her life for the better. She left the course and changed direction, applying instead to Goldsmith's College in London to take a degree in English and Drama.

Malorie was overjoyed to be accepted onto the course, but decided to take off a year first. She wanted to earn some money to help pay for her studies by working in computer software. As things turned out, Malorie loved her computing job so much that she then decided to study computer science at Thames Polytechnic, and did not take up her place at Goldsmith's.

2:15 AM

MALORIE'S STORY

MALORIE IS NOT AFRAID OF CHANGE. SHE IS CONSTANTLY LEARNING NEW THINGS AND IN THE LAST COUPLE OF YEARS ALONE, HAS LEARNT HOW TO PLAY THE PIANO, DRUMS, PRODUCE MUSIC AND EVEN TO SPEAK MANDARIN!

Malorie believed she could have a successful career in computing if she worked in the field. She studied hard at night, while holding down her computing job by day, and after three years she got her Higher National Certificate (HNC) with distinction.

MALORIE ON HER CAREER: 'I GUESS THERE'S A PARALLEL UNIVERSE SOMEWHERE IN WHICH I STILL COMMUTE INTO THE CITY OF LONDON EVERY DAY AND BEAT MY BRAINS OUT IN THE FINANCIAL SECTOR. AND THEN THERE'S ANOTHER UNIVERSE IN WHICH I ENDED UP AS AN ENGLISH TEACHER SOMEWHERE.'

What if you had to become a criminal to clear your dad's name?

HACKER
malorie **blackman**
Author of the award-winning NOUGHTS & CROSSES

What if you had to crack a code to save a life?

A.N.T.I.D.O.T.E
malorie **blackman**
Author of the award-winning NOUGHTS & CROSSES

Because Malorie's first proper job was in computing, many of her stories and characters also centre around the world of computers. The children in the stories Dangerous Reality, Hacker and A.N.T.I.D.O.T.E use many types of technology, particularly computers, to help them solve problems and find the answers to questions.

After completing her HNC, Malorie's computing career went from strength to strength. She quickly gained promotions and became a manager with a large, international firm called Reuters. However, despite her success, Malorie could not stop thinking about writing. She had never forgotten her first love and continually wondered what might happen if she turned her hand to storytelling again. Eventually, the temptation to write became too strong, and Malorie picked up her pen once more.

MALORIE ON HER CAREER CHANGE: '… IN MY MID 20S, AFTER A FEW YEARS IN COMPUTING, I DECIDED THAT I WOULD MAKE STRENUOUS EFFORTS TO BECOME AN AUTHOR. I THINK TRYING AND FAILING IS FAR BETTER THAN NEVER HAVING THE GUTS TO TRY AT ALL.'

Writing Again

When Malorie began to write again, she was very clear about the issues she wanted to talk about in her books. Having experienced racism growing up, and seeing how few novels featured black children, she was driven to write about black characters. Malorie was also inspired to write by great black authors she admired, such as Maya Angelou and James Baldwin.

Malorie worked hard, sending off her stories to publishers and receiving rejection letter after rejection letter. However, she never gave up, and one day she received the news that she had been waiting for. A publisher loved her stories, and wanted to publish them. Malorie's dream had finally come true!

MALORIE ON WRITING: 'I DON'T BELIEVE YOU CAN BE A WRITER UNLESS YOU HAVE A FEEL FOR THE WAY WORDS PLAY TOGETHER ON THE PAGE. AND THE WAY YOU GET THAT IS TO READ – VORACIOUSLY!'

Maya Angelou

MALORIE ON HER CHARACTERS: 'I GENERALLY MAKE MY MAJOR CHARACTERS BLACK BECAUSE THAT'S WHO AND WHAT I AM. BUT THE ETHNIC IDENTITY OF MY CHARACTERS IS NEVER THE WHOLE STORY.'

Malorie's path to becoming a writer proves that success does not always come immediately. Malorie had a whole host of day jobs before she became a full-time writer, including being a computer programmer, software specialist and database manager. Before that she worked in department stores such as BHS and Littlewoods as a Saturday girl. She also worked as a catering assistant, a receptionist and a typist. The worst job she ever had was as a kitchen porter – she only lasted for a day and a half because she hated it so much!

2:15 AM

MALORIE'S STORY

MALORIE HAS SOME GREAT ADVICE FOR BUDDING WRITERS: 'READ, READ, READ. THEN WRITE ABOUT WHAT INTERESTS YOU, NOT WHAT YOU THINK MIGHT MAKE MONEY. FIND YOUR OWN STYLE, DON'T COPY ANYONE ELSE AND DON'T GIVE UP.'

Not So Stupid!

With her writing career finally taking off, Malorie decided to improve her writing skills and signed up to a workshop for creative writing for children. There she learnt how to use her natural talent to its best effect.

Until she was sure that her writing career was going to be a success, Malorie kept her job in computing. She would write at night, then get up in the morning to travel to her daytime job. It was a proud moment for Malorie when her first story collection, *Not So Stupid!*, was published in 1990, to great reviews.

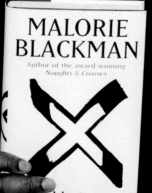

MALORIE BLACKMAN
Author of the award-winning
Noughts & Crosses

Double Cross

Malorie attends a book signing event for one of her best-selling novels, *Double Cross*, in 2008.

MALORIE'S STORY

MALORIE HAS PROVED THAT YOU NEED BOTH DETERMINATION TO SUCCEED AND BUCKET-LOADS OF TALENT TO BECOME A SUCCESSFUL AUTHOR. YOU HAVE TO BELIEVE IN YOURSELF AND NEVER GIVE UP. MALORIE'S FIRST COLLECTION OF STORIES, NOT SO STUPID!, WAS REJECTED BY MORE THAN 80 DIFFERENT PUBLISHERS BEFORE IT WAS FINALLY ACCEPTED AND PUBLISHED BY A PUBLISHING HOUSE CALLED WOMEN'S PRESS.

Feeling confident that she could be a successful writer, Malorie decided to finally give up her job in computing and devote all of her time to writing. Over the next few years she wrote many successful children's books, including Hacker, Operation Gadgetman and Pig Heart Boy.

So far, Malorie has written more than 50 books for children. Here are just some of them:

1990: *Not So Stupid!*
1992: *Hacker*
1995: *Operation Gadgetman!*
1996: *A.N.T.I.D.O.T.E*
1997: *Computer Ghost*
1997: *Pig Heart Boy*
1998: *Words Last Forever*
2000: *Tell Me No Lies*
2001: *Noughts & Crosses*
2003: *An Eye for an Eye*
2004: *Cloud Busting*
2005: *Checkmate*
2007: *Unheard Voices*
2010: *Boys Don't Cry*
2013: *Noble Conflict*

MALORIE ON READING: 'I REALLY WANT TO BE A VOICE FOR CHILDREN'S BOOKS, STORIES AND FOR READING. READING IS SO VITAL. IT'S A SKILL THAT ENRICHES AND ENABLES. READING ALLOWS YOU TO BE INFORMED AND IT GIVES YOU LIFE CHOICES.'

Riding on a high after the success of her first published books, Malorie decided to go one step further and write a film script! She applied to the National Film and Television School in London to learn how to write for films.

Malorie's first film script, *Play Time*, was based on her own experiences of bullying and feeling like an outsider as a teenager at school. The main character in *Play Time* is bullied by another girl, just as Malorie was. In Malorie's film, the heroine wins through in the end and overcomes the girl who is bullying her. Like Malorie's books, the film was a hit.

'I TRY TO WRITE EVERY DAY. THIS IS A JOB (ALBEIT A JOB I LOVE), NOT A HOBBY!'

'I PLAY THE PIANO AND THE DRUMS (NOT AT THE SAME TIME). I ALSO READ, COMPOSE MUSIC ON MY COMPUTER AND PLAY WORLD OF WARCRAFT! (I'M A LEVEL 90 WARLOCK!)'

Malorie has proved that she can turn her hand to almost any style of writing. Along with being an award-winning author and scriptwriter, Malorie has also written for television. She has written episodes of *Byker Grove*, and dramas for CITV and BBC Education.

Malorie's love of all things imaginative and creative can be seen in the way she chooses to spend her free time. She watches television, and goes to the theatre and the cinema. She loves music and has learnt to play several musical instruments. Malorie is a busy lady!

MALORIE SPEAKING ABOUT WRITING ABOUT HARD-HITTING ISSUES FOR TEENAGERS: 'WE NEED TO STOP UNDERESTIMATING OUR TEENS. IF WE DEFER ... "GRITTY ISSUES" UNTIL AFTER THE TEEN YEARS, THEN WE DO OUR TEENS A HUGE DISSERVICE. IF WE WANT MATURE, RESPONSIBLE TEENAGERS MAKING GOOD DECISIONS ... THEN WE HAVE TO EXPOSE THEM TO THE COMPLEXITY OF THESE SUBJECTS EARLY ENOUGH TO MAKE A DIFFERENCE.'

PRIZE-WINNING AUTHOR

'WRITING KEEPS ME SANE!'

Malorie has received rave reviews for her work from fellow authors, publishers and teachers. Today, she has a list of prizes to her name and many of her books have won awards, including *Hacker*, which won both the Young Telegraph/Gimme 5 Children's Book of the Year award and the WH Smith Mind Boggling Award in 1994.

In 2008, Malorie was given an OBE for services to children's literature. In 2013 she was made Children's Laureate – one of the greatest honours an author can receive.

2:15 AM

MALORIE'S STORY

MALORIE HAS EVEN BEEN NAME-CHECKED IN THE SONG WRITTEN IN THE STARS BY TINIE TEMPAH!

'I'M NOT REPRESENTATIVE OF ANYTHING. I'M JUST MALORIE BLACKMAN – A BLACK WOMAN WRITER.'

Today, Malorie continues to be one of the UK's most-loved children's book authors, and we can look forward to a future filled with many more of her stories. Here are just some of her awards and achievements:

A list of awards won by Malorie

1994: Young Telegraph/Gimme 5 Children's Book of the Year Award, *Hacker*

1994: WH Smith Mind-Boggling Book Award, *Hacker*

1996: Young Telegraph/Fully Booked Children's Book of the Year Award, *Thief!*

1997: Stockport Children's Book Award, *A.N.T.I.D.O.T.E*

2000: BAFTA, *Pig Heart Boy*, best drama

2004: Nestlé Smarties Book Prize (Silver Award), *Cloud Busting*, 6-8 years category

2004: Fantastic Fiction Award, *Noughts & Crosses*

2008: Awarded an OBE

2013: Made Children's Laureate

#1

MALORIE ON BEING CHILDREN'S LAUREATE: 'THE BEST THING ABOUT THE LAUREATE IS THAT I FEEL I'M GIVING SOMETHING BACK. IF I CAN GENERATE SOME PUBLICITY REGARDING CHILDREN'S BOOKS, READING AND LITERACY, AND CONTRIBUTE TO A DEBATE REGARDING THE WAY OUR CHILDREN READ THEN THAT'S WONDERFUL.'

How Well Do You Know Malorie Blackman?

1. What is the name of Malorie's daughter?
- a) Amy
- b) Elizabeth
- c) Julia

2. Where did Malorie's parents come from?
- a) Germany
- b) Venezuela
- c) Barbados

3. What was Malorie's favourite childhood book?
- a) The Lion, the Witch and the Wardrobe
- b) The Silver Chair
- c) The Tiger Who Came to Tea

4. What was Malorie's worst-ever job?
- a) Receptionist
- b) Kitchen porter
- c) Hair stylist

5. Which company published Malorie's first book?
- a) Bloomsbury
- b) Collins
- c) Women's Press

6. What was the name of Malorie's first published book?
- a) Not So Silly!
- b) Not So Slow!
- c) Not So Stupid!

7. Where did Malorie first go to college?
- a) Hull
- b) Huddersfield
- c) Henley

8. What field did Malorie work in before she became a full-time writer?
- a) Catering
- b) Careers advice
- c) Computing

9. How many books has Malorie written?

a) More than 10
b) More than 100
c) More than 50

10. What illness was Malorie wrongly diagnosed with?

a) Sickle-cell anaemia
b) Parkinson's disease
c) Leukaemia

Answers

1 b) Elizabeth
2 c) Barbados
3 b) *The Silver Chair*
4 b) Kitchen Porter
5 c) Women's Press
6 c) *Not So Stupid!*
7 b) Huddersfield
8 c) Computing
9 c) More than 50
10 a) Sickle-cell anaemia

Read about Malorie Blackman:

Malorie Blackman by Verna Wilkins (Tamarind, 2008)

Read some of Malorie's books

Noughts & Crosses (Corgi Childrens, 2006)

Pig Heart Boy (Corgi Childrens, 2004)

Find out more about Malorie at:

www.malorieblackman.co.uk/index.php/malorie-blackman

Quote sources

Page 4 Books for Keeps; **Page 7** Q&A With Malorie, Random House, 2013; **Page 8** www.malorieblackman.co.uk; **Page 9** (top) www.malorieblackman.co.uk, (bottom) www.wordpool.co.uk; **Page 12** Books for Keeps; **Page 15** The New Black Magazine; **Page 17** Books for Keeps; **Page 19** (top) www.malorieblackman.co.uk, (bottom) www.malorieblackman.co.uk; **Page 20** www.malorieblackman.co.uk, (bottom) www.malorieblackman.co.uk; **Page 21** www.malorieblackman.co.uk; **Page 22** www.wordpool.co.uk; **Page 23** www.malorieblackman.co.uk; **Page 24** www.wordpool.co.uk; **Page 25** (top) www.malorieblackman.co.uk, (bottom) www.malorieblackman.co.uk; **Page 26** (top) www.malorieblackman.co.uk, (bottom) Books for Keeps; **Page 27** www.malorieblackman.co.uk

Glossary

character
A fictional person in a story

commute
A daily journey to work from home and back again

discerning
To recognise things of value

discriminate
To make unfair rules and judgements about a person, for example, based on their colour

distinction
Notable, or a very high award

empathy
Understanding another person's emotions

enriches
To make richer, or to add to

ethnic identity
The culture, background and religion that a person identifies with

fiction
Stories, not fact

insidious
Deeply embedded, hard to get rid of

mythical
From myths, or stories

plot
The events in and structure of a story

prejudice
An unfair attitude towards something or someone

racism
Negative attitudes towards people based on their colour

strenuous
Difficult and tiring

theme
A concept or idea

voraciously
Eagerly

Index

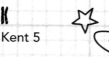